CELEBRITY SECRETS

INTERNET SENSATIONS

LIZ GOGERLY

WAYLAND

First published in 2012 by Wayland

Copyright © Wayland 2012

Wayland
338 Euston Road
London NW1 3BH

Wayland Australia
Level 17/207 Kent Street
Sydney, NSW 2000

Editor: Louise John
Designer: Emil Dacanay
Picture Researcher: Shelley Noronha

Picture Acknowledgements: The author and publisher would like to thank the following for allowing their pictures to be reproduced in this publication:
Cover and 4 Dave M Benett/Getty Images; 14 Robin Marchant/Getty Images for Sephora; 15 Jeffrey Ufberg /Getty Images for Lancome; 19 Dave Hogan/Getty Images. 5 Michael Bowles /Rex Features; 9 BDG/Rex Features; 18 David Fisher/Rex Features; 22 (top) Richard Young/Rex Features; 23 (bottom) KPA/ZUMA/Rex Features. 6 Starstock/Photoshot; 8 Derek Ross/LFI/Photoshot; 23 (top) JOY E SCHELLER/LFI/Photoshot. 7 John Shearer/WireImage for MTV.com. 10, 11 (Julie Bergin/Featureflash), 20, 21, 22 (bottom), 23 (middle) Shutterstock. 22 (middle) Photo © Jodie Rivera. 12 and 13 Photos © Dane Boedigheimer: 16 and 17 Photos © Simon Tofield /Canongate Books.

British Library Cataloguing in Publication Data

Gogerly, Liz.
    Internet sensations. – (Celebrity secrets)
    1. Celebrities–Biography–Juvenile literature.
    2. Internet entertainment–Juvenile literature.
    I. Title II. Series

004.6'78'0922-dc23

ISBN-13: 9780750267779

Printed in China

Wayland is a division of Hachette Children's Books, an Hachette UK company

www.hachette.co.uk

Disclaimer:
The website addresses and information included in this book were valid at the time of going to press. However, because of the constantly changing nature of the Internet, it is possible that some of the addresses may have changed or new content may have been posted on websites and social networking sites that the publishers cannot be accountable for. In preparation of this book, all due care has been exercised with regard to the suitability of the information presented. While the author and publisher regret any inconvenience any changes may cause to readers, neither the author or the publisher can accept responsibility for any such changes.

Contents

Bip Ling

FASHION 'IT' GIRL

Bip Ling celebrates at the launch of Sunglass Hut's new Covent Garden store, 2011.

Bip is now a big 'It' name in fashion. She has her finger firmly on the fashion pulse and has a fun and creative sense of style!

Stats!

Name: Bipasha Elisabeth Ling

Date of birth: 23 June 1989

Internet highlight: In 2008, Bip started her own blog at bipling.com.

Career high: Bip signed to Storm Models in 2011 and in the same year, became the British face of the American store 'Forever 21'.

Personal life: Bip is a regular on the front rows at fashion shows but her own life remains pretty private. She is close to her little sister Evangeline who is also signed to Storm Models.

Secret of success: Bip's mantra is 'every day is a style day'. And it is Bip's colourful and imaginative clothes that have turned her into a fashion sensation and woman to watch!

Bip's First Blog:

SATURDAY 20 DECEMBER 2008
My name is Bipasha Ling, I am known as Bip. I am 19 at this time and day of the year. I think this blog of mine is probably a good idea - too much goes on in my life, I don't take note of it - so here we are! Bip's blog!

Life Story

One night in December 2008, Bip Ling started a blog. The young Londoner with a love of fashion wanted to tell everyone about her passions in life. Bip loves everything from the colour pink to My Little Pony and cool tunes to gorgeous gowns. Her blog is filled with beautiful places, fashionable faces and playlists to get down to. It wasn't long before Bip was in the blog spotlight and big-time fashion industry insiders were following her every move...

Bip makes an appearance at the Roberto Cavalli fragrance launch in London, January 2012.

Art, fashion and creativity have always been part of Bip's world. Bip's parents were both studying at London's trendy Central Saint Martins when she was born. As a girl, Bip was always off to art and fashion events with her parents. Tanya, Bip's mother, made a name for herself as a fashion illustrator and her father William started the Fashion Illustration Gallery in London.

After studying art herself, Bip worked for Rough Trade Records and dabbled in PR. Bip loves music, too, and word soon got out about what a great DJ she is. These days she runs The How, a popular club night in Hoxton, London. Bip also spins tunes at trendy venues, festivals and fashion events!

Questions and Answers

Q What would you like to do next?

A "I'd love to do a TV show. It'd be similar to my blog with lots of interviews, but it'd be more art-based... I'm really keen for the interviews to be very chilled and conversational – then we'd just edit to any key parts. I'd also quite like to design a denim line but let's see how it goes."

http://www.vogue.co.uk/news/2011/02/23/bip-ling-secures-two-major-fashion-campaigns

Q Why do you think you're like a pony?

A "I am a pony because I have long hair, and I like to do my make-up in a My Little Pony style – black eyeliner and that..."

http://www.rosieishappy.blogspot.com/2011/05/bip-bip-move-over-chung.html

OK Go

VIRAL VIDEO STARS

OK Go at Summit Entertainment's world premiere of The Twilight Saga: New Moon, held in California, November 2009.

In 2005, OK Go made their first synchronised dance video. The video of *'A Million Ways'* was made in the back yard for about US $30!

Stats!

Name: OK Go

Date of birth: 1998

Band members: Damian Kulash (lead singer, guitar), Dan Konopka (drums), Tim Nordwind (bass guitar), Andy Ross (guitar, keyboards).

Albums: *OK Go* (2002), *Oh No* (2005), *Of the Blue Colour of the Sky* (2010), *180/365* (2011).

Internet highlight: In 2006, OK Go uploaded a video onto YouTube of the band doing its nifty synchronised dance routine across eight treadmills for the song *'Here It Goes Again'*. Six days later, over 1 million people had watched the video.

Career high: The *'Here It Goes Again'* video earned the band a Grammy award for Best Short Form Music Video and a YouTube award for Most Creative Video.

Secret of success: OK Go don't follow the rules of other bands. The band enjoys the freedom of making experimental and artistic videos and putting them out on the Internet. Nobody tells them what to do and they like it like that!

Life Story

OK Go was started by a couple of childhood mates. Lead singer, Damian Kulash, and bass guitarist, Tim Nordwind, met at school and formed The Greased Ferrets. Andy Duncan became drummer (replaced in 2005 by Andy Ross) and Dan Konopka joined up when they met at college.

OK Go had a big following before they were an Internet sensation. They had a record deal with EMI and two popular albums. Then, in 2005, the band started synchronised dance routines. At concerts they would suddenly throw

OK Go performing the famous treadmill routine for 'Here It Goes Again' at the MTV awards in 2006.

Questions and Answers

Q Why do you make music videos?

A "What we want to do with our videos is have a short burst of feeling; to give you a cool little world to live in for three minutes. That's what we're going for."

Damian Kulash, OK Go. http://www.spin.com/articles/qa-ok-gos-damian-kulash

Q What is the secret of your success?

A "We don't take ourselves too seriously but we take what we do really seriously and I think that shows."

Andy Ross, OK Go. http://www.guardian.co.uk/music/2011/jun/26/ok-go-music-videos-band-interview

down their instruments and start dancing. It really got the audience's attention! They took the idea a step further in the video for 'A Million Ways'. The video looked amateur but that was part of its appeal.

Next came the 'treadmill' video for 'Here It Goes Again'. It was so famous that a version was featured on 'The Simpsons' show. Since then, the band has created 'This Too Shall Pass' – an art installation that was inventively set to music. In the video for 'White Knuckles', the band starred alongside 14 dogs in a routine that took them 12 days to master. In the video for 'All Is Not Lost', the band wore blue leotards and danced on plexiglass so that they could be filmed from underneath. They were even asked to re-make the 'The Muppet Show' theme song. What will OK Go do next? You can bet you'll never guess!

Lucas Cruikshank

KID POWER!

Lucas Cruikshank smiles for the cameras at the Teen Choice Awards in California, 2009.

Lucas' own voice has to be digitally edited to get that high-pitch whiny voice for which Fred is famous.

Stats!

Name: Lucas Alan Cruikshank

Date of birth: 29 August 1993

Internet highlight: Lucas created the character of Fred Figglehorn back in 2006. In April 2008, he set up the YouTube Fred channel. The first Fred video was 'Fred on May Day', and Fred's channel went on to attract more than 1 million subscribers, becoming the first channel on YouTube to make it past a million!

Career high: In 2009, Lucas played Fred in the American sitcom 'iCarly'. The same year, he won the Teen Choice Award for Choice Web Star. His break onto the big screen was in 2010 with 'Fred: The Movie'.

Personal life: Lucas comes from a big family – he has two brothers and five sisters!

Secret of success: Lucas likes to focus on the fun side of things in life and doesn't let his critics put him off. He tries not to think too much about how many subscribers or how many hits he might have.

Life Story

Lucas and his co-star Jennette McCurdy have fun on the 'Fred: the Movie' film set in 2009.

Lucas Cruikshank is probably better known as Fred, the character he made famous on YouTube and at the movies. But, there's much more to this rising star than a high-pitched voice and tantrums…

Lucas lives in the small town of Columbus in Nebraska, USA, but would really like to move to Los Angeles to pursue other acting roles. When he was growing up, he'd borrow his mother's camera, and on his thirteenth birthday, he got his own digital video camera. He began writing and joined forces with his cousins Jon and Katie Smet to produce short videos. They started their own YouTube channel called JKL Productions.

Lucas reckons the character of Fred is based on his crazy little brothers. Fred is a six-year-old who throws tantrums, whinges and wings his way through everyday life in a comical fashion. Typical episodes include Fred going grocery shopping and spending over US $2,000 or Fred attempting to eat frozen pizza!

Questions and Answers

Q Where do you get the ideas for your next video in the series?

A "Usually it just comes to me randomly. I never sit down and try to think of a video idea. That doesn't really work for me…"
http://www.shineon-media.com/features/interviews/lucas-cruikshank-exclusive-interview

Q What is your advice to anyone hoping to make it on YouTube or as an actor?

A "Just have fun with it… I think you should do it for fun because you love creating and acting, just making people laugh."
http://www.shineon-media.com/features/interviews/lucas-cruikshank-exclusive-interview/

The Fred character was Lucas' way of poking fun at the vloggers on YouTube who talk about every little thing going on in their lives. Fred may have started out as a joke but, in 2009, Lucas made 'Fred: The Movie'. The sequel 'Fred 2: Night of the Living Fred' was released in 2011. A starring role in the film 'Emo Boy' is apparently in the pipeline. The word is out that Lucas is working on a new Nickelodeon show called 'Marvin, Marvin', too.

Justin Bieber

POP INTERNET SENSATION

Justin Bieber at the 2011 VH1 Do Something Awards, Hollywood.

Justin uses the social networking sites Twitter and Facebook to stay in touch with his fans. In 2011, Justin had **11** million followers on Twitter and over **20** million fans on Facebook.

Stats!

Name: Justin Drew Bieber

Date of birth: 1 March 1994

Internet highlight: Justin was discovered by accident on YouTube by his manager Scooter Braun in 2008. In 2010, the youngster was proclaimed the most Googled name on the planet.

Career high: Singing for President Barack Obama at the White House at Christmas 2009.

Personal life: Justin loves girls and his female fans go wild for him. 'Bieber fever' is a global phenomenon. However, Justin prefers to date other famous people.

Secret of success: Fame can be a lonely game. Justin manages to stay grounded by surrounding himself with close family and friends. On tour, he regularly hangs out with his old school mates, Ryan and Chaz. Justin also has a strong Christian faith.

Life Story

Justin Bieber is probably the first person many people think about when they hear the words 'Internet sensation'. The Internet literally launched his career and it helps to keep him at the top of the fame game.

Justin was born and grew up in Ontario, Canada. As a young child, music was an important part of his life. He listened to soul music and taught himself the guitar.

Questions and Answers

Q What is your ideal world?

A "I want my world to be fun. No parents, no rules, no nothing. Like, no one can stop me."

http://www.interviewmagazine.com/music/justin-bieber

Q You first started getting attention after you posted clips of yourself singing on YouTube. Why did you do that?

A "I was in a singing competition and my friends and family that couldn't see the competition wanted to be there, so I posted videos on YouTube and sent all my family the links... Then other people started watching it."

http://www2.macleans.ca/2009/12/15/macleans-interview-justin-bieber

When he was 12, Justin's mother, Pattie, began uploading videos of him onto YouTube. Justin belted out classics like 'Fallin'' by Alicia Keys. He was soon getting thousands of hits.

Justin's future manager Scooter Braun watched him by accident on YouTube. He flew Justin out to Atlanta to record a demo. In 2008, Justin was signed to R n' B superstar Usher's record label. Justin's first single 'One Time' wasn't a major hit, but 'Biebermania' soon caught on.

In 2010, Justin's debut album 'My World 2.0' topped the charts in the US, Canada, Australia and New Zealand. He was also voted Artist of the Year at the 2010 American Music Awards. Since then, the pop sensation has had international hit singles, released the film 'Justin Bieber: Never Say Never' and sold out arenas around the world. Justin has always kept in touch with his fans using Twitter and Facebook and uses the Internet to add to the 'Bieber fever'!

Pop Internet sensation Justin Bieber performs live in concert at the Nokia Theatre in Los Angeles, California.

Dane Boedigheimer

THE FACE BEHIND THE FAMOUS FRUIT

Dane believes the Internet and television are finally starting to cross paths – he has big hopes of bringing his Internet creations to the TV screen!

Dane has made lots of other talking food videos for his Daneboe channel on YouTube. 'Kool-Aide Man' was a viral hit before 'The Annoying Orange'.

Stats!

Name: Dane Boedigheimer

Date of birth: 28 September 1978

Internet highlight: In 2009, Dane uploaded the first 'The Annoying Orange' episode. The Annoying Orange channel was launched in 2010 and has become the eighth most subscribed to channel on YouTube. In 2011, the crazy citrus had notched up 9 million fans on Facebook and over 200,000 followers on Twitter.

Career high: Dane reckons he was speechless when he held the prototype toy of The Annoying Orange for the first time: "It really felt the character was real and had come to life. Kind of brought the kid out in me."

Personal life: Dane shares the YouTube channel SuperBoeBros with his younger brother, Luke. Check out the site for video game reviews. Meanwhile, we may not know who Dane is dating in real life, but The Annoying Orange loves Passion Fruit!

Secret of success: The Annoying Orange may be cheesy but those bad puns make many people laugh. Dane dreamed up The Annoying Orange in bed. He says he laughed out loud just thinking about it, and that's how he knew he had a winner.

Life Story

Who would think you could squeeze so much fun out of an orange? Not even Dane Boedigheimer thought his irritating creation would be so popular. The first The Annoying Orange episode was intended to be the only one. Since 2009, Dane has uploaded over 100 episodes. And Dane reckons there's plenty of juice in the talking fruit yet...

Dane is from North Dakota, USA. He studied film at Minnesota State University Moorhead. After working as a production assistant for MTV in California, he set up his own video production company, Gagfilms. Dane has been making short videos ever since, but it is The Annoying Orange that has brought him fame and fortune.

The Annoying Orange is filmed in Dane's own garage. The star of the show is the crazy orange with an annoying voice and irritating laugh (voiced by Dane). Dane superimposes his own mouth and eyes on to the character, too. Most episodes involve the orange insulting other pieces of food and end with the unfortunate food being sliced by a knife or squished in a food blender!

In 2011, Dane began working on The Annoying Orange spin-off for television. Expect to catch the juicy fruit on the Cartoon Network in 2012. "It's an exciting time to be involved in it all," Dane says. "I'm glad to be along for the ride."

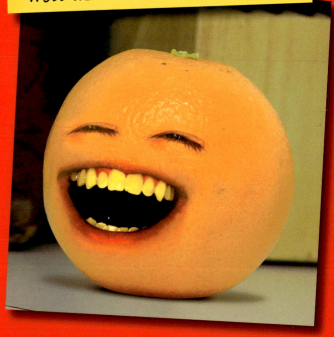

The Annoying Orange character features Dane's own eyes and mouth, as well as his voice!

Questions and Answers

Q Are you surprised how successful you have been?

A "Two years ago, when I launched The Annoying Orange, I never imagined that my unhealthy obsession with talking fruit would become such a phenomenon."

http://www.animationmagazine.net/tv/cartoon-network-to-squeeze-the-annoying-orange

Q What makes The Annoying Orange so appealing?

A "Everyone knows someone kind of like orange who is annoying, but somewhat lovable. Plus, there's just something funny about watching someone be annoyed."

Dane Boedigheimer, Variety, November 2011.
http://www.variety.com/article/VR1118046031

Michelle Phan

THE BEAUTY GURU

Michelle Phan attends Fashion's Night Out at Sephora in New York, September 2011.

Michelle uploads vlogs on the RiceBunny channel on YouTube giving advice to girls. This is her very own charity channel and each month, a different charity receives the profits from the channel.

Stats!

Name: Michelle Phan

Date of birth: 11 April 1987

Internet highlight: In 2011, Michelle had over 700,000 fans on Facebook and nearly 225,000 followers on Twitter, but it is her make-up tutorials on YouTube that have caused a sensation. She uploaded her first beauty video in May 2007, and to date has more than 200 videos on the site. Currently, she is the number one most subscribed to female on YouTube.

Career high: In 2010, Michelle joined the team at Lancôme becoming the beauty company's first-ever video make-up artist. "Lancôme is legendary, so I was shocked when they reached out to me," says Michelle. "I'm very excited about the things we'll be doing together." You can watch some of her videos on the Lancôme website.

Personal life: Michelle claims to have a strong spiritual side and goes to church regularly. She says she's just a regular girl who loves her family and friends.

Secret of success: Michelle's philosophy is to open your eyes and ears and take inspiration every day. People say she's a self-made woman, but she thinks nothing would have been possible without family and fans.

Life Story

Michelle Phan has turned applying make-up into an art form. On her YouTube channels, she posts tutorials to inspire and help other girls make the most of their looks. People call her a make-up guru, but she says her story is like Cinderella's...

Lancôme video make-up artist Michelle Phan has her own make-up done during her first appearance at Fashion's Night Out.

Michelle was born in Massachusetts, USA, to Vietnamese parents. Michelle's mother was a manicurist, so Michelle spent many hours as a girl in the beauty salon where her mother worked. Michelle's father worked in construction but he was a gambler. The family were regularly evicted from their homes and moved around. Life was a struggle. At school, Michelle was teased because she was Asian. At home, there wasn't a television so instead Michelle got into drawing.

Michelle was studying at Massachusetts College of Art and Design when she began her own blog. Many of her fans wanted to know how she achieved her natural look. She was inspired to get out her camcorder and record a video tutorial to teach her beauty secrets. Michelle has a distinctive soothing voice and she added relaxing music to the background. The video was an instant winner with her fans and Michelle has now created over 200 tutorials from her 'Romantic Valentine Look' to the Lady Gaga 'Poker Face' Tutorial.

Michelle never trained as a make-up artist, but these days she's in demand at fashion shows and Oscar parties. For Michelle, the job with Lancôme is a fairy tale ending.

Questions and Answers

Q **What are your goals?**

A "My goals from the start have always been to create quality content and empower young women. If I can accomplish these two goals, then that is worth more than anything in the world to me."

Michelle Phan, Forbes, September 2011
http://www.forbes.com/sites/michaelhumphrey/2011/09/21/michelle-phan-on-beauty-bob-ross-and-future-success/2

Q **What is the secret of success on the Internet?**

A "The Internet opens a lot of doors to those who are passionate."

Michelle Phan, St Petersburg Times, August 2009.

Simon Tofield

TOP CAT

Simon Tofield shares a close moment with his famous animation 'Simon's Cat'!

In 2008, Simon made a short video called 'Simon's Sister's Dog Fed Up' for the **RSPCA**. This greedy dog gobbles up all the food that falls on the floor at a dinner party.

Stats!

Name: Simon Tofield

Date of birth: 9 June 1971

Internet highlight: The feline fluff ball that is 'Simon's Cat' was first unleashed on YouTube in 2008. Since then, 'Simon's Cat' has picked up a global following with over 100 million hits on YouTube and more than 500,000 fans on Facebook.

Career high: The first 'Simon's Cat' film, 'Cat Man Do', won Best Comedy in the British Animation Awards for 2008. In 2009, 'Simon's Cat' starred in his very own book, which became the top-selling humour book in the UK that Christmas.

Personal life: In real life, animator Simon has four cats called Teddy, Hugh, Maisie and Jess. He reckons that all his cats have inspired the creation of 'Simon's Cat'.

Secret of success: 'Simon's Cat' is true to a real cat's life. Simon loves watching his own cats and many of his pets' antics end up on the films. He reckons that when fans say 'Simon's Cat' is like their own cat, this is the best compliment he could get.

Life Story

If you're a cat lover then the chances are you already know about 'Simon's Cat'. The sneaky, cheeky cat is not just an Internet sensation. Creator Simon Tofield has also penned two books, 'Simon's Cat' and 'Beyond the Fence', and contributes a regular comic strip to the UK Daily Mirror newspaper. On top of this, there is 'Simon's Cat' merchandise and an iPhone app called 'Purrfect Pitch'.

Questions and Answers

Q Where do you get your inspiration for 'Simon's Cat'?

A "I have three cats – Hugh, Maisie and Jess – [Simon currently has four cats] and they've all contributed to the films and the book. The good thing about having three cats is that if one is sleeping all day, there are two more to watch and they're always doing funny things."

http://articles.latimes.com/2009/nov/27/entertainment/la-etw-bookside27-2009nov27

Q Which animators have inspired you?

A "There are a lot of other talented artists I really admire. I especially like Calvin and Hobbes by Bill Watterson, as well as The Far Side series by Gary Larson."

http://bookhugger.co.uk/2009/11/simon-tofield-one-man-and-his-cat

Simon Tofield always wanted to make his own cartoon book. At film school, he taught himself animation, but never expected to become famous for it! Simon is now a director of London-based animation studio, Tandem. One day, while he was practising using an animation program for making short films, he decided to make a small film based around his own cat' antics. The short film was called 'Cat Man Do' and is about a hungry cat seeking attention from its owner. Soon afterwards, one of Tandem's clients uploaded the film onto YouTube. Within two days, there had been 60,000 hits and the 'Simon's Cat' phenomenon was born!

Simon has now added more than a dozen films to the series. These films may be short and simple but they have captured the hearts of millions of fans!

'Simon's Cat' was inspired by Simon's experience of living with his own four cats.

Charlie McDonnell

TOP TEENAGE VLOGGER

Charlie McDonnell at the British Academy Television Awards at the London Palladium, 2010.

Charlie is pretty much a grade **A** student. He got three **A*s**, seven **As** and one **B** in his GCSEs.

Stats!

Name: Charles Joseph McDonnell

Date of birth: 1 October 1990

Internet highlight: Charlie's YouTube channel charlieissocoollike has a massive international following. Not only did it become the most subscribed to channel on YouTube in the UK, but it was also the first British channel to get one million subscribers on the site.

Career high: Charlie was just 17 when his video 'How to be English', with instructions to make a cup of tea, was shown on the Oprah Winfrey Show in the USA.

Personal life: Charlie has thousands of female fans and the big question is has he got a girlfriend? Charlie keeps this side of his life private but in one of his song lyrics he pretends, 'That Hayley G Hoover is my girlfriend', in reference to one of his fellow YouTube contributors!

Secret of success: 'Enjoy what you do and always try to do it better!' Charlie reckons that he likes the new things he's working on the most. He's always pushing his creativity and trying to make his latest video the best one yet.

Life Story

Charlie McDonnell is like the big brother you never had! He's often in his bedroom and he's usually up to something. However, this young guy isn't just hanging out, he's making videos and vlogs that are watched by people all around the world. And, when he isn't up to that, he's picking up his ukulele and writing songs, too.

Charlie comes from Bath in Somerset. He never set out to become a vlogger but, in early 2007, he set up an account on YouTube.

Questions and Answers

Q What's it like being watched by so many people on the Internet?

A "It's hard to wrap my head around the fact that over a million people are watching the stuff that I make on the Internet… I try to make my videos more personal, like I'm speaking to one person rather than a big audience."

Charlie McDonnell, *The Sunday Times*, September 2011.

Q What advice would you give to other Vloggers?

A "… make sure that you have something to talk about… Most of all, don't try too hard, and be yourself."

http://survivethenet.blogspot.com/2009/07/interview-with-charlie-mcdonnell.html

The original plan was to make a video with a friend to upload to the site. When this didn't happen, Charlie got out his £50 camcorder and began vlogging. At first, he didn't get many hits but one day, he was featured on the front page of the UK site and he picked up 4,400 hits in just two days.

Charlie's popularity has been growing steadily ever since. Over the years, his subscribers have met his mum and little sister and watched him open his GCSE results. They've also watched him take on some pretty disgusting challenges posted by his fans. Top videos include Charlie eating fishfingers with custard and drinking the revolting home-made 'Charlie-Shake'.

Charlie has recently moved to London to pursue a media career. He has no idea where this will lead but one thing is for sure, he'll let us know in his next vlog!

Rebecca Black

CONTROVERSIAL CYBER STAR

Rebecca Black attends the Glee 3D premiere, Los Angeles, USA, 2011.

Rebecca has already appeared in Katy Perry's video. Now, she would love to do duets with Justin Bieber and Lady Gaga.

Stats!

Name: Rebecca Renee Black

Date of birth: 21 June 1997

Internet highlight: Rebecca's debut single 'Friday' has kicked up a cyber storm like no other. Unfortunately, it's the negative reaction to the video that has made it such an Internet sensation.

Career high: Love her or hate her, Rebecca's first single 'Friday' reached the charts in the USA, Australia, Canada, the UK and New Zealand. She has also appeared in the video for Katy Perry's single 'Last Friday Night (T.G.I.F.)'.

Personal life: Rebecca achieved instant stardom at the age of 13. Family and friends help to keep her grounded: "Just being able to be myself around them all the time is just really nice."

Secret of success: 'Friday' has to be one of the most talked about singles of 2011. Even bad press has been great publicity for Rebecca. Determination and courage have helped her to succeed, too. Sometimes, it's been difficult to handle critics but Rebecca has bounced back with another single, 'My Moment'.

Life Story

There is no doubt at all that Rebecca Black's debut single 'Friday' launched her as an instant Internet sensation.

Rebecca was born in Anaheim, California, USA. Both of her parents encouraged her love of music and her mother paid ARK Music Factory US $2,000 to record the single and video of 'Friday', a song about partying. Rebecca's voice was heavily auto-tuned and the video shows Rebecca zipping around in a convertible car.

'Friday' was uploaded to YouTube in February 2011. Within a month, there had been 1,000 hits but most people hated it and criticised the repetitive lyrics. Before long, 'Friday' was the hot topic on Twitter and by March, the video had gone viral. The response was negative, but Lady Gaga

Rebecca poses under a billboard in Los Angeles, USA, advertising 100 million YouTube hits for her debut single 'Friday'.

reckoned Rebecca was a 'genius'. Simon Cowell said: "Anyone who can create this much controversy within a week, I want to meet."

In less than a year, life changed dramatically for Rebecca. She left school, released her second single, 'My Moment', on her own label RB Records and then sang live on the results show for 'America's Got Talent' without auto-tuning. Rebecca is now making her first album and looking for a record deal!

Questions and Answers

Q **What was it like getting so many 'dislikes' on YouTube?**

A "When I first saw all these nasty comments I did cry. I felt like this was my fault and I shouldn't have done this and this is all because of me. Now I don't feel that way."

http://www.dailymail.co.uk/news/article-1378865/Rebecca-Black-police-protection-receiving-death-threats.html

Q **Which celebrity would you choose to be like?**

A "I really love how Katy Perry has done her whole career. And it probably seems like I'm saying this because I worked with her, but I've always been such a fan and really loved how she's handled things. Katy Perry has been a huge inspiration to me."

http://www.parade.com/celebrity/celebrity-parade/2011/08/rebecca-black.html

OTHER INTERNET SENSATIONS

Jodie Rivera

Career

Background: On YouTube she is known as VenetianPrincess. Jodie picked that name because she loves Disney princesses! As a girl, she adored singing and acting and even studied opera.

Internet fame: Jodie began making videos in her bedroom. In 2006, she uploaded the first episode of The Princess Chronicles onto YouTube. Jodie is now better known for her comic sketches of music videos.

Career highs: In 2008, Jodie's parody of Miley Cyrus' '7 Things' went viral with 3 million views in a month, making it one of the top-ten viral videos of the year. In 2009, Jodie won the title Miss YouTube.

Quote: "I can't express how grateful I am to have a career that I truly love. I get to connect with people all around the world. People watch me in their offices, schools, homes, etc. I am truly blessed to have such a large platform to reach people."

Website: http://www.vprincess.com/about

Basic Information

Home: Florida, USA.

Birthday: 22 April 1984

Julie Powell

Career

Background: Julie graduated in 1995 in theatre and fiction writing. After seven years of office jobs, she decided to start a blog. In 2002, Julie began her famous The Julie/Julia Project.

Internet fame: Julie's plan was to cook the 524 recipes from cookery writer Julia Child's Mastering the Art of French Cooking in just one year! Her blog attracted a massive online following.

Career highs: Julie's first book Julie and Julia: My Year of Cooking Dangerously was published in 2005, and became a bestseller in the USA. In 2009, it was made into a film.

Quote: "Two years ago, I was a 29-year-old secretary. Now, I am a 31-year-old writer. I get paid very well to sit around in my pyjamas and type on my ridiculously fancy iMac, unless I'd rather take a nap. Feel free to hate me – I certainly would."

Website: http://www.juliepowell.blogspot.com

Basic Information

Home: New York, USA.

Birthday: 20 April 1973

Jessica Lee Rose

Career

Background: Jessica was born in the USA but moved to New Zealand when she was eight. After studying in Auckland, she moved back to the USA in 2005. Soon afterwards, she enrolled at the New York Film Academy in Los Angeles to study acting.

Internet fame: Jessica's big break was playing Bree in the video blog lonelygirl15 in June 2006. The cool and kooky vlogs of teenager Bree soon became the most subscribed to channel on YouTube. However, what many of the fans didn't know was that Bree wasn't actually real and that Jessica was acting!

Career highs: The lonelygirl15 scandal didn't put a stop to Jessica's acting career. She's appeared in the US TV series 'Greek', movies and has also had several web TV roles.

Quote: "I'd love to be doing fun, goofy movies, feel-good movies that make people laugh and make people happy. I'd love to do some dramatic pieces later on."

Website: http://www.facebook.com/officialjessicarose

Basic Information

Home: Los Angeles, USA.

Birthday: 26 April 1987

Lily Allen

Career

Background: As a child, Lily was passionate about music. She went to about 13 different schools, a few of which she was expelled from! Eventually, Lily left school at 15 and began writing song lyrics. In 2005, she signed to Regal Recordings and began making an album.

Internet fame: In 2005, Lily uploaded some demos of her songs, including Smile and LDN onto Myspace. Before long, she had thousands of online followers. Lily became one of the first female performers to gain notoriety through the Internet.

Career highs: Lily went on to gain popularity, hosting her own TV show, but in 2010, she announced a break from her music career to concentrate on her family. Since then, she has launched the fashion boutique 'Lucy in Disguise' and has written lyrics for a stage version of Bridget Jones's Diary.

Quote: "My boyfriend gets really angry. He's like: 'I want to spend some time with you, do we have to have one and a half million people in the room with us?'"

Website: http://www.lilyallenmusic.com

Basic Information

Home: The Cotswolds, UK.

Birthday: 2 May 1985

Lana Del Rey

Career

Background: Elizabeth Woodridge Grant is her real name but she is known in the music world as Lana Del Rey. Lana spent her teenage years at boarding school before studying metaphysics at university. Lana reckons lots of people, from Frank Sinatra and Elvis Presley to Eminem and Britney Spears, have influenced her sound.

Internet fame: She's been called the 'Internet it-girl'. Her good looks and retro sound have certainly captured the attention of her many online fans. Her debut single 'Video Games' went viral in 2011.

Career highs: Lana's second solo album 'Born to Die' was one of the best-selling records of 2012. It reached number one in the UK and number two in the USA. In January 2012, Lana signed up to Next Model Management and she was the cover girl of the March 2012 issue of UK Vogue.

Quote: "I just put that song [Video Games] online a few months ago because it was my favourite. To be honest, it wasn't going to be the single but people really responded to it."

Website: http://www.lanadelrey.com

Basic Information

Home: New York, USA.

Birthday: 21 June 1986

Beckii Cruel

Career

Background: Rebecca Anne Flint, who is better known by her stage name Beckii Cruel, is a British pop dancer and singer. Beckii reached popularity in Japan after her YouTube videos were posted around the Internet.

Internet fame: In 2007, Beckii began a YouTube channel under the name 'Bextah', which was her childhood nickname. By 2010, Beckii was the seventeenth most subscribed user in Japan on YouTube. Her YouTube account soon reached 14 million upload views and over 51,000 subscribers.

Career highs: In August 2010, BBC Three produced a documentary about Beckii's story and she finally got the UK audience she wanted. Beckii is also a singer and former member of the band 'Cruel Angels'. She has released several singles, and is now recording her own album.

Quote: "It is a lot easier for me singing in English, as it's my natural accent, as opposed to my not-so-brilliant Japanese accent!"

Website: http://www.beckii.co.uk

Basic Information

Home: Ramsey, Isle of Man, UK.

Birthday: 5 June 1995

More Internet sensations to look out for

The Mini Band

Kev Jumba

Talking Twin Babies

Mysteryguitar Man

Fleur DeVlog

Talking Animals

Nyan Cat

Meet the Sloths

Index